This book belongs to

_____

_____

_____

MY 12TH GRADE STORY

Copyright © 2020 by Jean Lee

Cover Design by Jean Lee

MY 12TH GRADE STORY

My Full Name:

My Birthday:

Name of My School:

School Address:

School Website/Social Media:

School Mascot:

School Colors:

School Song(s):

My First Day of 12th Grade:

My Last Day of 12th Grade:

My Graduation Date:

My Class Rank:

My Overall GPA:

Date I Started This Journal:

What do you remember about your very first day of 12th grade? Were you scared? Excited?

Did all of your friends from 11th grade enter 12th grade with you? Did any new students enroll in your grade?

Were you friends with kids from other grades or other schools this past year?

What was your 12th grade homeroom? Who was the teacher, what days did you attend, and what did you do during homeroom?

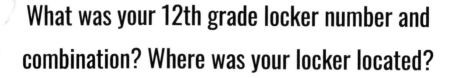

What was your 12th grade locker number and combination? Where was your locker located?

What classes did you take in 12th grade? Who were the teachers for each class?

Which 12th grade class was your absolute favorite? Who was your favorite teacher?

Which 12th grade class was your least favorite? Who was your least favorite teacher?

What were your grades for each class during 12th grade? What was your end-of-year GPA?

What extracurricular activities did you participate in during 12th grade? Do you wish you'd participated in something that you didn't?

Did you perform in any school plays, concerts or talent shows during 12th grade?

Were you involved in any activities unrelated to school such as church, clubs, organizations, etc. during 12th grade?

Did you eat lunch on or off campus during 12th grade? What was your go-to lunch this past school year?

Were you ever tardy during 12th grade? Did you ever get detention? Did you ever skip school?

How many days of school did you miss during 12th grade?
Was it due to illness or something else?

Did you have any medical issues during 12th grade? Any injuries or surgeries?

Did you take a foreign language in 12th grade? Are you now fluent? Do you wish you'd studied a different language?

Did you have P.E. in 12th grade? Did you have study hall?

As a senior, were there any special privileges for your grade? Late arrival or early release?

Did the school year end earlier for 12th graders over the other grades?

Who were your very best friends throughout 12th grade?

Did you have a falling out with any friends during 12th grade? Do you hope to reconcile with those people?

Did you get into any big fights during 12th grade? What were some of the biggest dramas that happened at school over the past year?

Did your school have spirit days this past year? If so, did you participate and what did you do? Dress up? Decorate your locker?

Did you win any awards during 12th grade? Were you hoping to win something that you didn't?

Did you attend any of your school's sporting events this past year? If so, which sports were your favorites?

Did you attend the school dances during 12th grade? If so, which ones and who were your dates for each?

Did you go to prom this past year? If so, what was the theme, where was it held, and who was your date?

What was the best day of 12th grade for you? What are your top five best memories of 12th grade?

What was the worst day of 12th grade for you? What are your top five worst memories of 12th grade?

Did you have any embarrassing moments during 12th grade? Are you still embarrassed or can you laugh about them now?

Were you in any relationships during 12th grade? Who did you date and for how long?

What did you and your friends like to do for fun, both after school and on weekends, during 12th grade?

What were the popular clothing styles that your classmates were into this past school year? How would you describe your style during 12th grade?

What were your favorite pieces and brands of clothing that you wore throughout 12th grade?

What were your favorite stores to shop at and things to buy during the past school year?

If you wore makeup during 12th grade, what were your favorite brands? Did you wear a lot of makeup to school or only on special occasions?

Did you have a part-time job during 12th grade? If so, where, what were your responsibilities, and how much money did you make per hour?

Did you have a car during 12th grade? Is so, what was the make, model and color? Did you drive yourself to school?

Did you get an allowance during 12th grade? If so, now much was it and did you have to do chores to earn it?

What vacations did you take during 12th grade? Did you go on vacation with family or friends?

What were your favorite movies of the past school year? Did you go to the theatre or stream films at home?

Who were your favorite movies stars from the past year? Were there movies stars you did NOT like that everyone else did?

What were your favorite television shows during the past year? Who was your favorite TV star?

Were there TV shows that everyone else seemed to love that you never watched? Which popular television stars did you not like?

Who were your favorite musical bands and artists from this past year?

What were your top five favorite songs that were released during your 12th grade school year?

Did you have a favorite artist or song this past year that no one else liked? Were there any popular artists or songs that you didn't like?

Did you attend any concerts this past year? Is so, where were they and who did you go with?

Did you have a cell phone during 12th grade? What kind? Did you text a lot? Play games on it?

What social media sites were you active on during 12th grade? Which site is your current favorite?

Did you like watching YouTube videos during 12th grade?
Is so, which channels and who were your favorite
YouTubers?

Do you have your own YouTube channel? If not, do you want one?

Did you play video games at all this past school year? If so, which ones and on what platforms?

What were some of the biggest entertainment stories this past school year? Any significant celebrity breakups or deaths?

What were some of the biggest news stories, both national and international, that occurred during this past school year?

Who were the Principal and Vice-Principal during your 12th grade year? Did you ever have any personal encounters with them?

Did you know any of the office staff at your school? Did you ever go to the offices for anything during 12th grade?

Who was your school counselor for 12th grade? What did you see them for? Did you like them?

Who were the US President and Vice President during your 12th grade year? Were there any big local, state or national elections?

Were you old enough to vote during 12th grade? If so, did you? Why or why not?

Who was the class and/or school president during your 12th grade year? What about the other offices (vice-president, secretary, etc.)?

Did you participate in student government during your 12th grade year? Why or why not?

Were you in any clubs during 12th grade? Did you serve on any committees?

What time did school start every morning? Were you early, on time or late?

What did you do in the two hours immediately after school got out this past year? Stay for activities, go straight home or go to work?

Did you do your homework every night or try to finish it right before class? On weekends, did you save homework for Sunday night?

Who lived at home with you during your 12th grade school year? Did you live at the same address the whole time? Did you have any pets?

Did any of your school classmates live in your neighborhood? What about kids from other schools who you became friends with?

What was your favorite food this past school year? What was your favorite fast food restaurant? Your favorite full-service restaurant?

What were favorite hot and cold drinks this past school year? Were you a coffee drinker? What was your favorite soda pop?

What were your favorite snacks, either at school or at home, during the past school year? Did you prefer sweet or savory treats?

Did you take any field trips or overnight trips with your 12th grade class or with other groups of students?

Over the past year, did you ever stay home alone for a night or longer while your parents were out of town?

How did you spend Halloween during 12th grade? Did you dress up? Go to any parties?

How did you spend Thanksgiving during 12th grade? What foods does your family always have on Thanksgiving?

How did you spend Christmas during 12th grade? What presents did you get? Did you have a stocking?

Did you exchange Christmas gifts with friends during 12th grade? If so, with whom and what did you give and receive?

How did you spend Valentine's Day during 12th grade?
Did you send or receive cards, flowers, or gifts?

How did you spend the Easter holiday during 12th grade?
Did you get an Easter basket?

Did your family observe any other holidays during your 12th grade school year?

How did you spend your birthday during 12th grade? How old did you turn? What gifts did you get?

How did you spend your 12th grade Spring Break? Was it a better or worse Spring Break than in previous years?

Was there a senior skip day this year? If so, did you participate?

Did anyone play any end-of-year pranks? If so, did you know about them in advance? Did you participate?

What was your graduation ceremony like? Where was it held? Were you nervous to walk across the stage?

Who was/were the Valedictorian(s)? Did you receive any special awards or scholarships?

Did you have a graduation party? What were the decorations and food like? How many people attended?

Did you get a year book? Did you have your friends sign it?

_____

_____

_____

_____

_____

_____

_____

_____

_____

_____

_____

_____

_____

_____

_____

_____

_____

_____

_____

_____

_____

What are you plans for this summer?

Are you going to attend college this Fall? If so, where and what do you plan on studying?

When did you start preparing for college? When did you take the SAT's or ACT's and what were your scores?

How many schools did you apply to? Was it hard to decide on which college to attend?

_____

_____

_____

_____

_____

_____

_____

_____

_____

_____

_____

_____

_____

_____

_____

_____

_____

_____

_____

_____

If you aren't attending college this Fall, what are your plans? Are you taking a gap year or do you want to go straight into the workforce?

If you are going away to college, will any of your 12th grade classmates be going to the same school?

Do you think you'll be homesick while away at college? How often do you plan to come home to visit?

Which friends do you hope to keep in contact with once you are all away at college?

Do you think social media will make it easy to maintain your high school friendships? Who will you continue texting with?

Which of your 12th grade classmates do you think will be the most successful? Who do you think will have a hard time after high school?

What is the biggest lesson you learned during 12th grade?

What do you consider to be your greatest 12th grade accomplishment?

What is your biggest regret about 12th grade?

Is there any one person you hurt during the 12th grade that you wish you hadn't? Have you made amends to them?

Who hurt you the most during 12th grade? Have you forgiven them?

If you could go back in time and give yourself advice before the first day of 12th grade, what would it be?

Where do you see yourself in five years? In 10 years? In 20 years?

_____

_____

_____

_____

_____

_____

_____

_____

_____

_____

_____

_____

_____

_____

_____

_____

_____

_____

_____

_____

_____

Do you think you'll attend future class reunions? Why or why not?

Are you happy that 12th grade is over?

What will you miss the most about your senior year of high school?

PHOTOS & MEMORABILIA

PHOTOS & MEMORABILIA

PHOTOS & MEMORABILIA

PHOTOS & MEMORABILIA

PHOTOS & MEMORABILIA

PHOTOS & MEMORABILIA

PHOTOS & MEMORABILIA

PHOTOS & MEMORABILIA

PHOTOS & MEMORABILIA

AUTOGRAPHS

AUTOGRAPHS

AUTOGRAPHS

AUTOGRAPHS

AUTOGRAPHS

AUTOGRAPHS

AUTOGRAPHS

AUTOGRAPHS

AUTOGRAPHS